EXTREME
WEATHER

WEATHER AND CLIMATE

EXTREME WEATHER

Terry Jennings

Evans

First published 2005 by Evans Brothers Limited
2A Portman Mansions
Chiltern Street
London W1U 6NR

British Library Cataloguing in Publication Data
Jennings, Terry J.
Extreme Weather.- (Weather and climate)
1. Weather - Juvenile literature
2. Climatology - Juvenile literature
I. Title
551.5'5

ISBN 0237527499

Designer: Giraffic Design
Editor: Mary-Jane Wilkins
Illustrator: Graham Rosewarne
Series consultant: Steve Watts

Picture acknowledgements
Corbis: page 2, 6 (top), 9 (bottom), 11 (bottom), 15, 17, 25, 29.
Ecoscene: page 9 (top), 20, 35 (top), 38 (top), 43 (bottom)
Terry Jennings: page 10, 11 (top), 30 (bottom), 32, 34, 43 (top)
Oxford Scientific: front cover, page 6 (bottom), 7, 12, 16, 21, 26,
37 (bottom), 40
Still Pictures: page 3, 14. 18, 19, 22, 23 (top and bottom), 24, 27,
28, 30 (top), 31, 33, 35 (bottom), 36, 37 (top), 39, 41, 42, 45

Contents

Weather and atmosphere

1

Today, floods, droughts, tornadoes, hurricanes and other weather disasters wreck people's lives all over the world, despite advances in technology. To understand the causes of extreme weather, we first need to know about the causes of more typical weather.

The ruins of a building battered by Hurricane Charley when it struck Florida in the United States in August 2004.

The peaks of the Chugach Mountains in Alaska, USA, are covered in snow all the year round because of their height and latitude.

The air around us

We live at the bottom of a sea of air called the atmosphere. It provides the air we breathe and insulates the Earth. It acts as a sunshade during the day, protecting us from excessive heat, and as a blanket at night, preventing the Earth from cooling too much. It filters out radiation from the Sun and makes meteorites burn up by friction before they hit the Earth. Nine-tenths of the atmosphere is in the layer from the ground up to about 16 km.

The layers of the atmosphere

The air surrounding the Earth has three main layers. The lowest, the troposphere, stretches up to about 16 km and contains 90 per cent of the mass of the air. The temperature here falls rapidly with increasing height, and at its upper limit is about −60°C. Most storms begin in the troposphere and great moving masses of air keep the clouds in motion. The stratosphere, the second main layer, reaches up to about 80 km. It has low concentrations of the atmospheric gases. Above is a belt in which the gases are even 'thinner' and their atoms are electrically charged, or ionised, by the Sun's radiation.

Air pressure and temperature

Although it is invisible, air has substance and consists of atoms and molecules – in the same way as liquids and solids. Air also has weight, and 1 cubic metre weighs about 1.25 kg. Because of this, air exerts a pressure on all the surfaces it touches. This is greatest at sea level, where it is equivalent to about 1 kg on every square centimetre. The higher you go, the lower the pressure becomes.

Air pressure varies and these changes can be recorded with a barometer and used to forecast weather in temperate (or middle) latitudes, ie those with neither very hot nor very cold climates. High pressure usually means fair weather, and when the barometer falls it is likely to rain. Temperatures on Earth vary hugely from place to place and are affected by altitude, latitude, land and sea, wind and ocean currents, clouds and relief.

The Sun doesn't heat air directly; it is warmed by the Earth. The Sun's rays heat the surface of the Earth and this radiates back the heat which warms the air. You feel a drop in temperature if you climb a mountain and move away from the source of the heat, the Earth's surface. The drop averages 2°C per 300m.

Temperature and latitude

Temperature also gradually drops the further away from the Equator you go. This is why there is permanent snow and ice in the polar regions, yet high temperatures in the tropics. These differences are caused by the fact that the Sun's rays strike the area away from the Equator with less warming power than at the Equator itself. Also, to reach the Earth's surface, the Sun's rays pass through the atmosphere

WEATHER MACHINE

The atmosphere is like a vast machine. The energy which drives the machine comes from the Sun, and it is also fuelled by air and water. The power the machine produces is shown as various types of weather, including winds, rainstorms, snowstorms and thunderstorms.

The weather on this island in French Polynesia is influenced by its distance from the Equator, as well as by the Pacific Ocean which surrounds it.

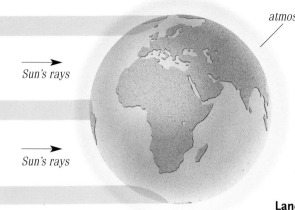

atmosphere

Sun's rays

Sun's rays

**THE EFFECT OF
THE CURVATURE
OF THE EARTH ON
THE SUN'S RAYS**

where much of their heat is reflected back by clouds and dust. The rays have to travel further to reach the poles than the Equator. The further they travel, the more heat they lose. This explains seasonal variations in temperature. Clouds also reduce the Sun's warming effect, causing variations in temperature.

Land and sea

As the Sun's rays strike the Earth they are absorbed by a very thin layer of the Earth's crust. By contrast, over the sea, the rays penetrate deeply and their heating power spreads further. The sea has to absorb more solar radiation than the land for its temperature to be raised by the same amount. On a sunny day, the land is much hotter than the sea. The land also loses heat more quickly, and cools down as fast as it warms up. So land surfaces can have great ranges of temperature, between night and day, and from season to season. The opposite is true of the sea.

Wind and ocean currents

Like the air of the atmosphere, the waters of the oceans mix and circulate. Warm water from the tropics flows towards the poles, and cold water from the polar regions flows towards the Equator. These currents may form a definite stream, such as the Gulf Stream, or they slow down and spread out to form drifts. Winds blowing over warm ocean currents are warmed. Warm air holds more water than cold, and warm winds blowing across the ocean pick up moisture from the surface. When they reach land they bring rain. Winds blowing over cold ocean currents to land are cooled. They do not hold much moisture and dry the land they pass over.

**THE WORLD'S
OCEAN CURRENTS**

Winds blowing over warm ocean currents are warmed, while those blowing over cold currents are cooled. Water takes between 500 and 2,000 years to make one complete trip around the world.

Warm currents

Cold currents

Cloud barriers

Clouds act as barriers to the Sun's radiation. The world's highest temperatures are recorded under the clear sunny skies of tropical deserts. Clouds also check the heat radiated by the Earth, so that cloudy areas tend to have a small daily range of temperature, compared with the hot days and cold nights of tropical deserts.

The shape of the land

The shape, or relief, of the land surface causes temperature variations. Vineyards and orchards are planted on the sides of valleys because heavy, cold air moves down slopes, and pockets of freezing air may lie in the valley bottom. Mountain villages in the Alps grew up on the north side of valleys because they receive more of the Sun's radiation there. Mountains can also restrict the circulation of air in the lower atmosphere. The Rockies restrict the penetration of warm, moist air from the Pacific Ocean, so the interior of North America has more extreme continental weather conditions.

Winds and pressure belts

The air of the lower atmosphere moves constantly, forming winds. The propelling force for this is heat energy from the Sun. As air is warmed, it expands and rises, forming low pressure areas. And as the warmer, lighter air rises, masses of denser, cooler air move in as wind to take its place. On Earth, the heat of the tropics acts like a radiator heating the air. This warm air is less dense, which makes it rise so that cooler air is drawn in from elsewhere to take its place. As a result, most winds that blow over the Earth move from the cold poles towards the Equator.

The rotation of the Earth swings the masses of air around faster at the Equator than at the poles, so the winds in the northern hemisphere are deflected to the east, and those in the southern hemisphere to the west. As the winds blow, local forces can override global ones. Land masses warm and cool more quickly than the sea, so new high and low pressure areas form at different times of the day in different seasons.

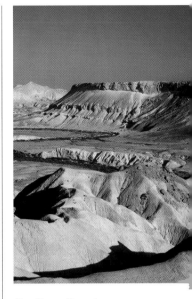

The Negev Desert in Israel. Temperatures are highest under the clear, sunny skies of tropical deserts like this.

High winds bend a tree photographed from inside the eye of a hurricane in Florida, USA.

Cumulonimbus clouds loom over Lisbon, Portugal. These towering clouds bring heavy rain and thunderstorms.

Water vapour in the air

The water vapour in the atmosphere is a gas, and the amount in the air depends on the temperature. The higher the temperature, the more water vapour the air can hold. When air is holding the maximum amount, it is saturated. Usually it is less than saturated, and the amount of water vapour is recorded as a percentage of the total possible, called relative humidity. Moist air does not have to be cooled much before it becomes saturated. If the air is cooled further, it can no longer hold the water vapour and it condenses into water droplets.

Millions of tonnes of water are carried in the atmosphere as invisible water vapour or clouds. Warm air carries more moisture than cold, so when warm air is cooled, it can no longer retain its water vapour. As it condenses around the tiny particles of dust, salt, pollen or plant spores in the air, the water vapour forms microscopic water droplets, light enough to float in the sky, where they form clouds.

There are three main types of clouds. Cirrus clouds are made of ice crystals at high altitudes (above 6,000m) and appear as thin, feathery streaks. Cumulus clouds are thick with a flat base and domes or billows above. Their bases are below 2,000m. Stratus is a layer of cloud with a base between the ground and 2,000m which may be hundreds of metres thick and bring drizzle or rain. Some clouds are mixtures of two types.

Rain, thunder and lightning

In temperate regions, rain starts at the top of clouds as ice crystals. Some melt and fall as rain and some freeze again after melting and become sleet or snow. In the polar regions cold air carries little moisture, so clouds are rare and there is little rain or snow. In the tropics, heavy rain falls most days. When rising warm moisture builds into thunderclouds, they become electrically charged. As the electricity discharges from one cloud to another, or from cloud to Earth, the current heats the surrounding air to white heat – a lightning flash. Instantly the air expands, and causes the sound waves of a thunderclap.

Snow and fog

At 6,000m and above, clouds are composed of ice crystals suspended in the air until they combine into snowflakes large enough to fall. They are six-sided, and no two are exactly alike. Many melt as they pass through warmer air on their way down, and reach the ground as sleet or rain.

Fog is produced when the air is saturated. As it cools, the water vapour condenses into droplets of water too small and light to fall. Fog is really a cloud at ground level. It may form when the ground cools at night and chills the damp air above it, or when warm moist air moves over a cold ocean current or cool land area.

Fog forming over farmland in Norfolk, England, as the ground begins to cool at the end of the day.

This satellite photograph shows a hurricane approaching the Gulf Coast of the United States. Satellites help forecasters to predict accurately where and when a hurricane will hit land.

Hurricanes

2

Hurricanes bring destructive winds, severe thunderstorms, vast quantities of rain and waterspouts. They force up seawater into devastating waves. They are the largest storms on Earth.

Hurricane Georges whips up the sea and drags at palm trees as it approaches Florida, USA, in 1998.

How hurricanes are formed

Every year about 60 huge storms develop over tropical oceans that generate speeds of more than 120 kph. The meteorological name for these is a tropical cyclone. In the west Pacific, north of the Equator, strong tropical cyclones are called typhoons. In the Indian Ocean and in the south-west Pacific Ocean they are known as cyclones. When they form over the Atlantic or eastern Pacific they are called hurricanes. In Australia these violent storms are called willy-willies.

Most hurricanes form within the doldrums, a narrow tropical belt between the north-east and south-east trade winds, where the temperature is over 24°C. The doldrums of the Atlantic are mainly north of the Equator, so the South Atlantic Ocean does not have hurricanes. By contrast, the Pacific doldrums extend both north and south of the Equator, so hurricanes occur in both these regions.

A hurricane forms when moist air is warmer than the surface of the ocean. Denser, colder air pushes underneath this warm, saturated air. The atmospheric pressure within the rising warm air drops sharply and the wind speed increases. The newly-formed storm picks up vast amounts of energy and moisture as it rushes towards land. The heat and water vapour often create violent thunderstorms. These may group together if the water is over 24°C and spin around as one large system. As they are pushed further across the ocean by the wind, the storms draw in more warm, moist air, gathering energy. They spin in ever-tighter circles, their speed increased by the Earth's rotation. When the wind speed reaches 120 kph the storm becomes a hurricane. Hurricanes can produce sustained wind speeds of 250 kph, with gusts up to 300 kph. Tornadoes produce stronger winds, but are short lived, whereas a hurricane can last for a week or two and cover thousands of kilometres.

The hurricane season
During the summer and autumn the ocean surface of the tropical regions and the air above it are warm. High winds evaporate the sea water rapidly, and the water vapour rises to form clouds. Large amounts of heat are released into the atmosphere by condensation, and this provides the energy that fuels the system. In the north-eastern Pacific and western Atlantic regions, the official hurricane season runs from 15 May to 30 November.

The structure of a hurricane
A hurricane can measure 400 km across. Inside, a swirling mass of winds spirals upwards. At the centre, or eye, of the storm, the skies are clear and temperatures are high. The calm eye may be 40 km across, but the strongest winds are immediately around it. The storms with the smallest eye are often the most powerful. Around the eye are thick, swirling clouds that tower 10 km above sea level. As this warm, moist air spirals upwards, the water vapour cools and turns to rain and releases the hurricane's energy.

INSIDE A HURRICANE

Winds spiral outwards

Bands of spiralling raincloud

Eye

Warm, moist air rises

Cars were wrecked, trees uprooted and buildings reduced to rubble when Hurricane Mitch struck Honduras in the autumn of 1998.

A hurricane takes several days to travel from the ocean where it was formed to land. As it roars by, it seems to someone on the ground that the storm has ended as the eye passes overhead. The wind and heavy rain of the hurricane are followed by clear skies and an unnatural calm. Within an hour or two, however, the eye passes and the other side of the hurricane hits, bringing more destructive winds and torrential rain.

Hurricane strengths

Every hurricane is classified according to its strength on a scale from 1 to 5. This helps people in its path to know how strong it is going to be, and to decide whether to board up windows, seek the safety of a storm shelter or to evacuate the area. The mildest hurricane is category 1 and has wind speeds of at least 120 kph. The strongest and rarest is category 5, with wind speeds faster than 250 kph. These are the most feared hurricanes. Hurricane Andrew, a category 5 hurricane in 1992, holds the record for being the most costly in American history. Hurricane Mitch, which hit Central America in autumn 1998, also reached category 5. The most recent was Hurricane Ivan, which reached category 5 over the Windward Islands in September 2004.

Hurricanes follow a curved path. At first they move west with the trade winds, but like all great air movements they are deflected in their path by the Earth's rotation. This is called the Coriolis effect. In the northern hemisphere a hurricane usually follows a north-westerly path. In the higher latitudes it then curves round towards the north-east. In the southern hemisphere a hurricane usually begins travelling south-west and then veers round to the south-east. Hurricanes travel at various speeds. Near the Equator the speed varies between 8 and 32 kph, but in the higher latitudes it can be as much as 80 kph.

HUGE ENERGY

Scientists estimate that a single hurricane can unleash more energy in a single day than 500,000 atomic bombs.

Hurricane damage

A hurricane can uproot trees and lift boats from harbours and fling them over harbour walls. Houses are destroyed as their roofs are torn off and large lorries lifted off the road. Cables and wires are ripped from their poles and anyone out of doors stands little chance of survival.

The force of the hurricane also pushes up huge waves on the sea. The water level near or under a hurricane can be five metres or more higher than the calmer seas around. These waves are called a hurricane surge. When they reach land they cause serious flooding. A hurricane surge may last only a few hours, but its crashing waves usually cause severe damage. Most deaths in a hurricane are from drowning.

Hurricane damage occurs mainly on islands and in coastal areas. The storm usually dies out fairly quickly once it is away from the ocean from which it takes its energy and moisture. The friction caused by the land also slows the winds so that they become less damaging.

Naming and studying hurricanes

An Australian meteorologist, Clement Wragge (1852-1922) was the first person to give hurricanes names. He chose the names of people from the Bible. Later, the United States Weather Bureau gave female names to hurricanes. Since 1978, meteorologists have drawn up a list of alternate boys' and girls' names, in alphabetical order. Every time a new hurricane is detected, it is given the next name on the list.

Meteorologists need to find out how hurricanes form so they can forecast them accurately, reduce the damage they cause, or even prevent them developing. Hurricanes are very difficult to study as they destroy scientific instruments and kill anyone who goes near them.

THE 2004 HURRICANE SEASON

A series of hurricanes battered the Caribbean, Florida, the Gulf of Mexico and the eastern coasts of the United States during 2004. Charley, Frances, Gaston, Ivan and Jeanne flattened thousands of homes. In Haiti, Jeanne caused flooding and mudslides which killed 2,000 people. Hurricane damage in Florida alone is estimated at $26 million.

A satellite photograph showing both Hurricane Frances (top left corner) and Hurricane Ivan (bottom right corner) over the Caribbean in the summer of 2004.

HURRICANE MITCH

In 1998 Hurricane Mitch swept over Honduras and Nicaragua. It killed more than 12,000 people in devastating floods and mudslides.

Flying through a hurricane

A few specially-strengthened military aircraft can fly through hurricanes to measure the wind speeds and directions, the location and size of the eye, and the air pressures and temperature changes within them. Scientists on board have reported that the heaviest rain falls in spiral bands. Inside the eye the air is pure and clear, while the surrounding clouds rise up in tiers. The water vapour inside the clouds instantly turns to ice on the aircraft's wings. There is a dome of clear blue sky high above the hurricane. Other aircraft, called hurricane hunters, fly around the edges of hurricanes and track their position.

A satellite photograph of Hurricane Linda which formed off the west coast of Mexico in September 1997.

The role of satellites

Satellites take photographs of storms as they grow. These help scientists to predict when a hurricane is going to develop and its likely path. They also record changes in the temperature of the ocean surface as a hurricane forms in the atmosphere. Satellites track every low pressure area that might lead to a full-scale hurricane. They send data to monitoring centres, such as the National Hurricane Center in Florida.

Forecasting hurricanes

There are several warning signs when a hurricane is approaching. First come dull red sunsets caused by a thin haze of clouds. The air becomes very hot and humid and the air pressure, as shown by a barometer, is high as the wind dies down. At sea there is a growing swell. As the storm approaches, the barometer needle drops suddenly, because the air pressure falls rapidly. A rain cloud rushes towards the land and torrential rain begins.

Injuries and deaths caused by hurricanes have been greatly reduced because of improved methods of forecasting. The hurricane which struck Galveston in Texas in 1900 was the most deadly disaster ever to befall the United States. Reaching speeds of about 170 kph, the hurricane is believed to have killed between 10,000 and 12,000 people. It caused an estimated $20 million damage.

More recently, Hurricane Andrew, which blasted its way across the Bahamas, the Gulf of Mexico, southern Florida and into Louisiana in August 1992, caused damage estimated at $26.5 billion. Andrew was about 800 km in diameter, but its fiercest winds, around the eye, gusted up to 320 kph. In the four hours Andrew took to cross Florida it destroyed 80,000 homes and damaged 55,000 more. It also destroyed 15,000 boats.

Television and radio broadcast alerts about the approach of the Hurricane Andrew allowed about a million people to flee north out of its path. Most of those who stayed went to a public hurricane shelter or were in concrete houses. So in spite of the record-breaking amount of damage Andrew caused, it killed fewer than 50 people.

A caravan park destroyed by Hurricane Charley in Punta Gorda, Florida, in August 2004.

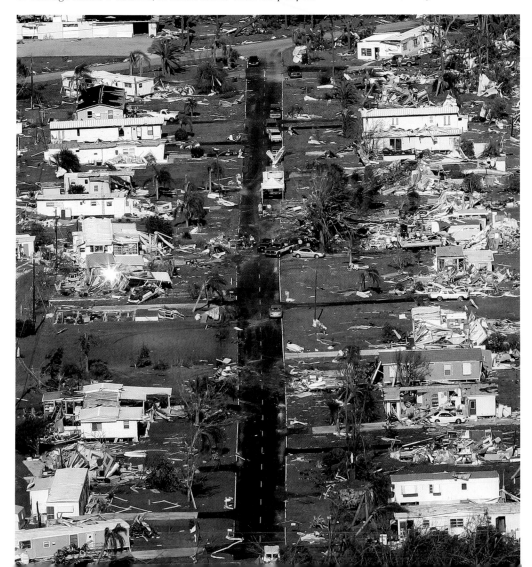

3

Tornadoes

Tornadoes are small, very powerful whirlwinds that form very suddenly. The word tornado comes from the Latin word *tornare,* meaning to twist or turn.

TORNADO DISASTERS

The swarm of tornadoes that struck the Madaripur district of Bangladesh in April 1977 killed almost 900 people and injured more than 6,000. Bangladesh was also the scene of the world's worst tornado disaster in 1989, in which 1,300 people died.

Where tornadoes occur

A tornado is smaller and faster than a hurricane, but can be more destructive, destroying everything in its path. It appears as a twisting funnel of cloud up to 200m high, stretching down from a storm cloud to Earth. A tornado travels at up to 120 kph. Inside the wind speed can reach 800 kph – the highest on Earth. It is impossible to be sure, because a tornado would destroy any wind-speed recorder. Tornadoes vary in size from a few metres across to more than 500m and can travel 200 km. They are strongest in the temperate latitudes where the effect of the Earth's rotation is greatest. The most violent ones happen in the US, which has about 1,000 a year. Tornadoes also blow up regularly in parts of Canada, Argentina, China, Australia, South-West Asia, the Indian subcontinent, and even Europe. The UK has between 15 and 30 small tornadoes each year.

A tornado over South Central Kansas in May 2001. Tornadoes commonly occur in the Great Plains area and the south-east of the United States.

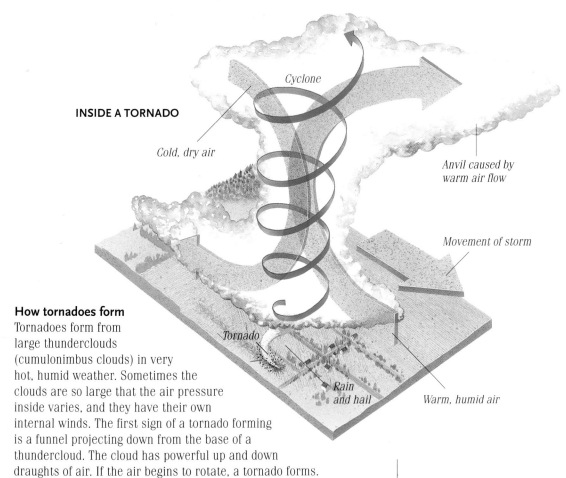

INSIDE A TORNADO

Cyclone

Cold, dry air

Anvil caused by warm air flow

Movement of storm

Tornado

Rain and hail

Warm, humid air

How tornadoes form

Tornadoes form from large thunderclouds (cumulonimbus clouds) in very hot, humid weather. Sometimes the clouds are so large that the air pressure inside varies, and they have their own internal winds. The first sign of a tornado forming is a funnel projecting down from the base of a thundercloud. The cloud has powerful up and down draughts of air. If the air begins to rotate, a tornado forms.

There are about 45,000 thunderstorms a day around the world, yet few spawn tornadoes. Instead, they usually produce heavy rain, thunder or hail. One sign of a forming tornado is dark patches of cloud, shaped like stubby fingers, hanging from the base of a thundercloud. These may grow until a funnel-shaped cloud hangs below the parent cloud. Many fade after about ten minutes, but sometimes the funnel grows. The cloud twists downwards faster and faster, until the funnel reaches the ground. At first the tornado is made up of tiny water droplets. But the moment the cloud touches the ground, it sucks up soil, sand, dust and other debris. That is why a tornado appears black.

Changing air pressure

Much of the damage caused by a tornado comes from the sudden changes in air pressure it creates. At the centre of the tornado, the air pressure is very low. This low pressure core acts like a powerful vacuum cleaner,

Damage caused by a tornado which struck Moore, Oklahoma in the United States. Neither cars nor homes are safe when a tornado strikes.

and tornadoes have been known to pick up lorries, horses, whole trees and even people. Buildings in the path of a tornado are likely to be badly damaged. The pressure inside the houses and other buildings it passes over remains normal. As the tornado passes over, the sudden drop in outside pressure causes the air inside the buildings to expand violently and the buildings explode like burst balloons.

Tracking tornadoes

The relatively small size and brief life of tornadoes (two-thirds last less than three minutes) makes them difficult to predict, but a kind of radar has increased the accuracy of tornado forecasts. Since 1977, Doppler radar has been used to detect the circular movements inside storms that can develop into tornadoes. The radar can predict a tornado about 25 minutes before it emerges from the base of the clouds. This allows just enough time to send out warnings. Better forecasting and communication is helping to save lives. Tornadoes killed about 100 people in the United States every year during the 1970s. By the 1990s this had fallen to 50.

A waterspout whirls over the estuary of the River Humber in England. Waterspouts cause much less damage than tornadoes.

Waterspouts

Waterspouts are rapidly rotating columns of air that form over water – usually a lake or a sea. They resemble tornadoes over water. They are never as severe as a tornado funnel on land, and the average wind speeds in a waterspout are about 80 kph. However, waterspouts do not need severe thunderstorms to set them in motion. The visible funnel of the waterspout is caused by water droplets that have condensed from the air because of the low pressure inside the spiralling waterspout.

Waterspouts need warm water to develop and are common in the Florida Keys in the United States. They also happen in coastal regions of the equatorial Atlantic and Indian Oceans, the Mediterranean and the Gulf of Mexico. Some are isolated, while others occur in clusters.

The first sign of a developing waterspout is often a shadow on the water where the rotating air is disturbing the surface. Once it has formed, the waterspout slowly follows a curved path. After about 15 minutes, cooler air enters the funnel of the waterspout, causing it to lose energy and disappear.

The highest waterspout recorded was seen in May 1898 off Eden in New South Wales, Australia. A reading taken with a theodolite from the shore showed it to be 1,528m high and about 3m wide. Waterspouts can be a hazard to small boats and sometimes they cause injury and loss of life.

Dust devils

A dust devil is an upward-swirling mass of dust-filled air varying in height from a few metres to over 300m. Unlike tornadoes, dust devils form from the ground up. When air near the ground becomes much warmer than the air above, it becomes unstable, begins to rise and draws more air in underneath it, sucking up dust in the process.

Dust devils resemble miniature tornadoes, but are very short-lived and much less damaging. They are common in hot, dry desert and semi-desert regions of the world, particularly Africa. In the Sahara Desert dust devils can last from a few minutes to a few hours, every day. In Tucson, Arizona, a desert city in the United States, there are about 80 dust devils every day.

A dust devil is an upward-swirling mass of dust-filled air. Dust devils are common in hot, dry parts of the world.

Thunderstorms

Thunderstorms happen on hot days when moist air close to the ground is heated and rises quickly. They are common in many parts of the world, and in some parts of the tropics thunderstorms occur most days in the rainy season.

LIGHTNING STRIKES

There is a saying that lightning never strikes the same place twice. But during one thunderstorm the Empire State Building in New York was struck by lightning 15 times in 15 minutes.

Air currents

An updraft may start over ground that has been heated more strongly by the Sun than the surrounding land. The rapidly rising air currents lead to the formation of towering cumulonimbus clouds with a characteristic anvil-shaped top. These thunderclouds may be only a few kilometres across and yet may tower 20 km into the sky.

Cloud to ground lightning photographed at night in Oklahoma in the United States. Only about one lightning flash in four travels from a cloud to the ground.

Inside a thundercloud, strong upward and downward air currents sweep ice crystals, ice pellets and water droplets past and into each other. These movements create static electricity that builds up in the cloud. Positive electric charges collect towards the top of the cloud and negative charges in the lower parts. They are strongly attracted to each other. Eventually the insulating layer of air between the two sets of charges cannot keep them apart any longer and a massive spark – lightning – is released as the charges neutralize themselves.

The lightning discharge is usually within a cloud or between clouds, or between a cloud and the air. Only about one in four lightning flashes travels from a cloud to the ground. Then the lightning is attracted to the higher parts of the Earth's surface. This is why lightning conductors are placed on tall buildings and why it is dangerous to shelter under a tree in a thunderstorm. One of the safest places to be in a thunderstorm is inside a car, as the tyres provide insulation.

Sprites

Until recently, aircraft were thought to be safe in a thunderstorm because they are not in contact with the ground and therefore cannot conduct electricity. But scientists recently discovered that lightning flashes, called sprites, are sometimes discharged from the top of a thundercloud towards space. These are suspected of causing a small number of aircraft crashes.

Two lightning bolts strike mountain foothills in Tucson, Arizona in the United States.

The sound of thunder

The temperature of a lightning flash is more than 22,000°C. It superheats the air around it, making it expand at an incredible speed and then contract equally rapidly. This creates the sound waves that we hear as thunder. Light travels faster than sound, so we see the lightning flash before we hear the thunder. The closer the thunderclap and lightning flash are to each other, the nearer the thunderstorm is.

Hailstones left after a thunderstorm. Large hailstones may contain many layers of ice and they can cause great damage to crops, greenhouses and cars.

Frozen hailstones

Because a thundercloud is so tall, its upper levels are well below freezing point. The rising air currents inside the cloud vary in strength. A raindrop on a strong rising current may be swept so high that it freezes, only to fall again as the air current weakens. At lower levels,

a frozen raindrop may collect more water which freezes on the next upward thrust. This process may be repeated many times. Hailstones with 25 layers of ice have been recorded. They can do great damage to standing crops, greenhouses and cars, as well as injuring people. The worst hail disaster on record struck India in 1888, when hailstones the size of cricket balls battered Moradabad, killing 246 people. In tropical areas, although hailstones are often formed in thunderclouds, they rarely reach the ground as the high temperatures melt them on the way down.

Floods

Floods can cause great damage and loss of life, although sometimes they can be useful. Flooding may be triggered when heavy rain or rapidly melting snow produces more water than a river can hold. Serious coastal flooding occurs when a strong wind blows towards the land during a high tide.

Why rivers flood

The most extreme flooding occurs in tropical regions, where seasonal winds called monsoons bring heavy rains. Many parts of the world have sudden, heavy rainstorms, especially places which have most of their rain during one short, wet season. The rain swells the rivers and can flood land far away.

A river may also flood if it becomes blocked. The long rivers that flow north to the Arctic Ocean in northern Canada and Russia freeze over in winter. When spring comes, the ice melts in the warmer parts of the rivers further south before it melts in the northern stretches near their mouths. The rivers fill up with the melted snow, but their mouths are still frozen. When the meltwater reaches the ice blockage, the rivers overflow and flood the land.

A girl wades through floods in Dhaka, the capital of Bangladesh. The city occupies a low-lying site on the Ganges delta and is flooded regularly.

*This aerial photograph
shows the River
Ganges snaking
towards its delta
over low-lying land.*

Rocks and flooding

Some rocks, such as chalk and sandstone, are permeable and soak
up water like a sponge. Other rocks, such as clay and granite, are
impermeable and they can help to make flooding worse because they
don't let water through. The water runs over their surface and quickly
fills up rivers and streams. Towns and cities have huge areas of tarmac
and concrete which act in the same way as impermeable rocks. Heavy
rain runs off these surfaces into drains, which flow into rivers and
streams. The sudden rush of water can make the rivers and streams
overflow and flood.

Useful floods

When a river nears the sea or a lake, it flows across flat lowland.
Here the river flows along slowly in huge curves called meanders.
This combination of flat land and wide meanders allows floodwater to
spread out across a large area of land. This area is called a flood plain.
When a river floods, water pours over its banks, dumping mud and
sand over the land. These make a very fertile soil, called alluvial soil.

Floods in Bangladesh

Most of the country of Bangladesh lies on a delta at the mouths of
the Rivers Ganges and Brahmaputra. This flat flood plain is one of the
largest in the world. The two great rivers often flood, leaving a layer
of fertile mud over the plain. So long as the monsoon rains fall, up to
three crops of rice are grown here in a year. However, in some years
the monsoon rains fail to arrive and when this happens there is a
drought and food shortage.

In other years, the rains are very heavy and the flooding is severe.
Too much water destroys the crops, and damages buildings, power
supplies and roads. In severe floods many people die.

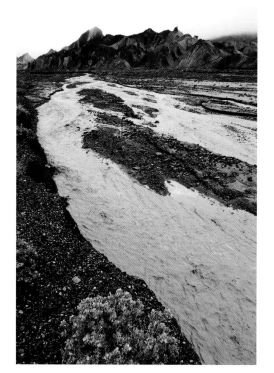

A flash flood caused by a thunderstorm over Death Valley in California, USA.

Flash floods

The most spectacular and rapid floods are flash floods. Most are caused when a thunderstorm or hurricane brings a short, heavy burst of rain over mountains. Then the water level in the mountain streams rises very quickly and sends a wall of water rushing as fast as an express train into the valley below. Other flash floods are caused by the rapid melting of snow, or when a dam bursts.

Thunderstorm floods

Although few thunderstorms last more than an hour or two, in that time they can release more than 100 million litres of water. This can cause huge unexpected flooding.

In August 1996, a severe thunderstorm hit the Pyrennees Mountains in northern Spain. The sky darkened and hailstones the size of golf balls fell. They were followed by 80 mm of rain in two hours. The rain washed soil, stones, boulders and trees into a mountain stream, which quickly became a raging torrent. Downstream, artificial drainage channels rapidly filled with water. Suddenly a giant wall of water crashed down the valley and through a nearby camp site. A total of 87 people died and 180 were injured. Some bodies were found 16 km from the camp site.

Desert floods

In many hot desert areas, the Sun bakes the ground hard like concrete. When there is a heavy rainstorm, the water rushes over the compacted surface, filling gullies and dry river beds in seconds. In the deserts of North America, more people drown in flash floods than die from thirst.

Bursting dams

Dam bursts are another major cause of flash flooding. A dam is a large wall or bank built to hold back the water in a river. A man-made lake, called a reservoir, fills up behind the dam. Dams are built across river valleys to store water for drinking, irrigating crops and producing electricity. They can even help to stop flooding by holding back the water that would otherwise inundate areas further downstream. But if a dam bursts, it can cause a devastating flood.

Temporary dams

Trees, rocks and other debris washed away by heavy rain can become trapped by a bridge, forming a temporary dam. The water level rises behind the dam until the dam and bridge eventually burst under the pressure of the water, resulting in a flash flood.

Flood disasters

Slow-rising floods often cause the most deaths and greatest destruction, especially in Asia. In China, if the monsoon rains last longer than usual or are heavier than normal, then flooding almost always follows.

During February and March 2000, flooding in Southern Africa killed hundreds of people and left about 1.25 million homeless. Mozambique bore the brunt of the flooding, but Zimbabwe, Botswana, Zambia and the island of Madagascar were also affected. The severe floods in Mozambique were caused by the extraordinary amount of rain that fell during February – 1,163 mm compared with the average of 177 mm. Rivers across the region burst their banks as Cyclone Eline swept in, bringing new rains to lands already waterlogged by more than two weeks of storms. Crops and village granaries were washed away, destroying food supplies, while roads, bridges and dams were destroyed. Mozambique was cut in two by a strip of muddy water 50 km wide and up to 5m deep. The flood left homes unfit to live in and drinking wells unusable. The floodwaters were contaminated by human sewage and malarial mosquitoes bred in the pools of stagnant water.

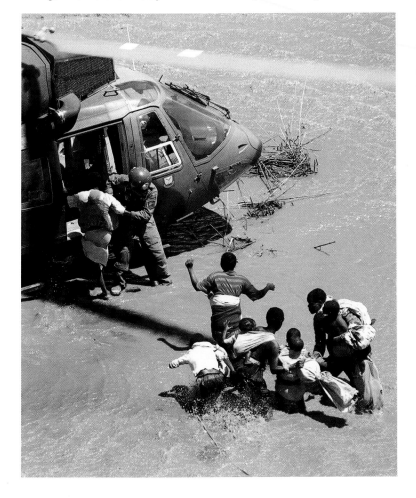

A helicopter belonging to the South African Army rescues flood victims from the banks of the Limpopo River in Mozambique.

Trees and flooding

In many parts of the world, wood is used for cooking, heating water and keeping warm. Trees are cut down to clear land for crops and provide animal grazing. Without trees the soil in which they grow is easily washed away. This is called deforestation.

In tropical climates, tree-covered slopes help to prevent flooding and mudslides. Forests on hillsides also stop fertile soils washing away. In the rainy season, tree roots soak up much of the water as it sinks into the soil. If the trees did not act as living sponges, the water would fill streams and rivers and make them overflow. The tree roots also hold the soil together. When forests are cut or burnt down there is nothing to hold the soil in place and it is washed away.

Storm surges and cyclones

Coastal floods can be caused by a storm surge. This sudden rise in sea level happens when water is piled up against the coast by strong winds blowing towards the land. The water may rise as much as 5m above normal levels and cause widespread flooding and loss of life. Surges are common in the Gulf of Mexico, along the Atlantic coast of the US, around the islands of the western Pacific and in the Bay of Bengal.

Bangladesh is often hit by cyclones. Only a quarter of the country lies more than 3m above sea level, yet 117 million people live there. In April 1991, the surface of the sea off Bangladesh was whipped up by a tropical cyclone until it was 6m higher than normal. This surge swept over low-lying areas of Bangladesh, killing 140,000 people and leaving millions more homeless. Six years later, another powerful tropical

A storm surge hits Western Samoa, a group of islands in the Pacific Ocean.

cyclone struck Bangladesh and damaged 400,000 homes. This time many lives were saved because better warnings had been given and people took refuge in cyclone shelters built after the 1991 disaster.

The Yangtze River

The Yangtze is the longest river in China and the fourth-longest in the world. More than 700 small rivers join it on its 6,300 km journey across China, and nearly half of China's 1.2 billion people live near its banks. In 1998 exceptionally heavy rain caused the river to flood. The floods were worse than usual because, over the years, the trees on the slopes above the river had been cleared. The river banks gave way, hundreds of villages were destroyed and millions of farmers were stranded on strips of higher ground. The flood affected 240 million people. About 3,000 were drowned and millions more left homeless.

Sinking cities

Many cities grew up around trading ports and lie close to sea level, which puts them at risk of flooding. Some are slowly sinking. In Bangkok, people take water from 10,000 wells under the city. As water is drawn from the wells, the rocks dry out and shrink, the city sinks, and is threatened by floods from the river and the Gulf of Thailand,

A similar disaster threatens the Italian city of Venice, by the Adriatic Sea. So much water has been taken from the ground that the city has sunk by more than 12 cm in 50 years. At the same time, the Adriatic Sea has risen by about 9 cm and Venice now floods whenever there is a high tide combined with heavy rainfall and a storm surge.

Floods in the Piazza St Marco, Venice, Italy. Because Venice is sinking, flooding is a common occurrence.

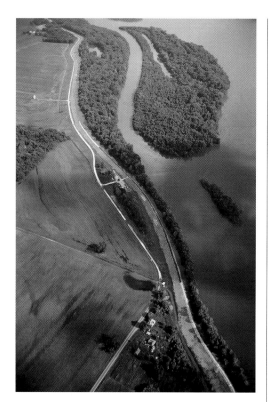

Flood waters breaking through a levee built by the River Mississippi, south of Quincy, Illinois, in 1993.

Protection from banks

A river carries huge quantities of mud and sand eroded from the sides and bottom as it flows from its source in the hills. In the lower course of a river, the water flows more slowly, and drops mud and sand, raising the river bed. This happens with the Mississippi River in the United States. As the river bed has risen, people nearby have built high banks, called levees, to stop the river flooding their homes. In places the levees are more than 6m above the level of the Mississippi.

Dredging river beds

Dredgers can remove mud and sand from a river bed to deepen the river so that it holds more water. Some rivers meander from side to side in their lower parts. This slows down the flow of water and can cause flooding.

Straightening the channel so the water flows out to sea more quickly can prevent flooding, though it might make a river less suitable for plants and animals. Sometimes a relief channel is dug to divert floodwater away from the main river. Planting trees on steep slopes near rivers slows down the rate at which water flows down the slopes and into the river. It also helps to hold the soil in place so it is not washed into the river.

MISSISSIPPI FLOODS

After months of heavy rain the Mississippi River broke through its levees in 120 places in 1927. It flooded 67,000 square km, 600,000 people lost their homes and 246 people died.

A dredger at work, removing mud and sand from the bottom of a river in Switzerland.

Dams and flood barriers

Some flooding can be prevented by dams or sluice gates. These hold back and store water in reservoirs and release it in a controlled way. There are disadvantages to constructing dams. The Aswan High Dam in Egypt holds back the waters of the River Nile in Lake Nasser, and controls the flooding of hundreds of kilometres of the Nile valley to the north. The water from Lake Nasser irrigates large stretches of land and supplies hydroelectric power to Egypt's industries. However, vast quantities of the water in Lake Nasser evaporate in the heat of the Sun, and much of the fertile mud which once spread over the fields during floods now clogs up the reservoir. The lake water is slightly salty and, when it evaporates, it builds up a layer of salt in the soil in which plants cannot grow. Now some areas of land downstream of the lake have become infertile.

Flood barriers are built across river mouths to protect towns and cities upstream from storm surges. To prevent storm surges from the North Sea flooding London, a barrier was built across the mouth of the River Thames. This is raised when surges and storm floods threaten.

The barrier built across the River Thames to prevent storm surges from the North Sea flooding London, England.

Coastal defences

The best barriers against flooding from the sea are beaches, sand dunes and salt marshes. These are all damaged by the growth of towns and resorts, and other human activities. Today huge sums of money are spent on building artificial sea defences. Sea walls of stone or concrete protect beaches and buildings. Most modern walls are curved to push the waves upwards and back out to sea again.

Breakwaters are long barriers of boulders or concrete built into the sea which protect harbours during stormy weather. However, they can sometimes redirect the damaging waves elsewhere. Groynes – fences on beaches at right angles to the sea – slow down water currents, preventing sand and pebbles from being washed away. In some places, artificial reefs – rows of rocks parallel to the coastline – are being built to reduce the power of the waves.

Soft engineering

Increasingly people are using 'soft engineering' techniques, such as planting marram grass, which is tolerant of salt, to prevent sand dunes being blown away. Improving the drainage of soft cliffs can help to prevent cliff falls caused by heavy rain. Allowing sea water to flood coastal land can actually protect against flooding inland. Salt marshes provide a rich habitat for birds, wildfowl, plants and other wildlife. Just as importantly, the marsh breaks the force of the waves, preventing flooding further inland.

Landslides and mudslides

Somewhere in the world a landslide is probably happening now. Landslides can be triggered by heavy rain, frost, melting snow or an earthquake, causing huge masses of rock, soil or mud to fall rapidly down a slope.

Ice and water

Many rocks are soft and porous, while others have many cracks in them. In cool, wet climates, the water that collects in these pores and cracks may later freeze. As the water freezes, it expands and the ice presses against the sides of each pore or crack. On high mountains, water often freezes at night and melts again next day. Eventually the ice widens the cracks in the rock until pieces begin to break off. Rainwater is slightly acidic and this acid slowly softens rocks such as chalk, limestone and even granite, so that pieces crumble away.

The effects of weathering

In hot, dry places, such as deserts, the heat during the day makes the rocks expand, while at night they cool and contract. This gradually weakens the rocks until pieces break off. Plant roots also break up rocks when they grow in cracks. As the roots grow they force the sides of the crack further apart, weakening the rock and splitting it. Burrowing animals can also widen cracks in rocks and weaken them.

A large bank of loose stones, called scree, at the bottom of a mountain in the Swiss Alps.

Sometimes pieces of rock slide downhill as soon as they break off, forming scree, but usually the pieces collect in one place until something starts them moving. This can be a natural event such as heavy rain, melting snow, an earthquake or waves from the sea. Human activities such as mining and quarrying can also set off a landslide.

Rock slides

One of the most extreme kinds of rock fall happens when a mass of rock thunders down a slope. Sometimes a layer of air is trapped under the falling rock, which then floats along like a high-speed hovercraft. Rock slides of this kind are much more dangerous than simple rock falls because they often occur on the lower slopes of mountains, near to farms and villages. Rock slides have killed many people and destroyed whole villages in the Canadian Rockies, Norway, Switzerland and many other mountainous areas.

Mudslides

Mudslides form when soil or other loose material on a slope becomes soaked with water. This usually happens after a sudden, heavy rainstorm or when snow melts rapidly on hills and mountains. Some mudslides are caused by rainwater or melting snow mixing with the ash from a volcano. The wet material then no longer sticks to the slope, but slides downhill, flowing like a liquid.

In May 1998 heavy rain in the hills around Naples in Italy washed thousands of tonnes of mud down into the valleys below. The mud came from hills where trees had been cut down or burned. The mud rushed down gullies like a tidal wave. It tore down houses and bridges and swept away cars and trees. Parts of some villages were buried under two metres of mud. When the rain finally stopped, the sun baked the mud hard, making rescuers' work more difficult. At least 81 people were killed and many more were injured.

Erupting volcanoes

Many volcanoes are so high that they are permanently covered in snow. If the volcano erupts, red-hot ash mixes with the melting snow and forms a very dangerous mudslide. This happened when the Nevado del Ruiz volcano in Colombia, South America, erupted in November 1995. The snow and ice on the volcano melted, and the water carried thousands of tonnes of ash as it rushed down the mountainside. One of the streams of mud was 40m high, and some travelled 60 km before they finally came to a halt. Altogether, the mudslides killed more than 23,000 people and destroyed thousands of homes.

A large rock slide beside the Colorado River in Utah, United States. Rock slides like this can be very dangerous if they happen near villages.

LARGEST LANDSLIDE

The world's largest landslide happened on the slopes of Mount St Helens in Washington State, USA, in May 1980. An earthquake triggered mudslides, landslides and floods which released 2.8 billion cubic metres of rock and mud. More than 259 sq km of forest were destroyed and about ten people were killed, along with countless elk, deer, bears and coyotes.

7

Drought

A drought is a long period of dry weather when no rain falls for weeks, months or even years. Parts of the world that have a dry season and a wet season expect drought every year. People plan for it by storing water and by growing crops that can withstand the dry weather. Drought is far worse when it is not expected.

The effects of drought

Drought makes lakes, rivers, reservoirs and wells dry up because more water evaporates than falls as rain or snow. Plants wilt and die. Animals trample the ground as they search for food and drink. If the drought is brief – a partial drought – many plants recover and the damage is not lasting. If it is long, winds may blow away the topsoil, plants may catch fire and most of them will not be able to regrow. If the rains fail in tropical areas, there is no water to store for the dry season. During a prolonged drought, with no crops for food, people starve unless they can find food elsewhere. In poorer parts of the world, drought brings famine, disease and huge numbers of deaths.

Catastrophic droughts

Drought is more severe in some areas than in others. The worst droughts happen in areas bordering the deserts of the world. Where warm, tropical air masses descend north or south of the Equator, they form an area of high pressure, or anticyclone, in hot desert areas. The clouds disperse and rainfall is minimal. The drying out process is made worse by lots of sunshine and low humidity. If the prevailing winds shift from their normal path, then the high pressure, anticyclonic conditions of the permanently dry regions spread to areas that usually have a wet season, and cause a drought.

The remains of a giraffe which died during a drought in Kenya. When plants wilt and die during a drought, plant-eating animals, or herbivores, quickly starve to death.

A southward shift of the prevailing westerly winds caused the most severe drought in the twentieth century. This was in the Sahel, on the southern fringes of the Sahara Desert in Africa, which normally receives low rainfall. During the early 1960s there was a series of good seasons and many people settled on the edge of the desert. Then at the end of the decade a drought began that has continued on and off ever since. It was widespread in 1984 and 1985, when it caused crop failures and famine in 20 countries. Ethiopia had had low rainfall and poor harvests for years, made worse by a civil war from which millions of people had been forced to flee. About half a million died there in 1985. Many scientists believe that the climate of the Sahara region is becoming drier as a result of long-term change. Over 10,000 years once-fertile grasslands have become the largest hot desert in the world.

A tribesman searches for water in the desert in Ethiopia during a prolonged drought.

Why the rains fail

Anything that interrupts the water cycle can produce a drought. Winds might change direction, taking rain-bearing clouds elsewhere. Sometimes an area of high pressure settles in one place for a long time. Then the air becomes very still and calm and rain clouds cannot form, which leads to a serious drought. Droughts can also be caused by quite small changes in the temperature of the surface of the sea, or higher than average air temperatures. If the surface waters become warmer, there is less evaporation of water from the sea and so fewer clouds form. An example of drought caused in this way is described in Chapter 9.

The dried-up Ladybower Reservoir in the Derwent Valley, South Yorkshire, England during a drought.

Man-made drought

People create drought conditions by disrupting the water cycle. The Aral Sea, on the borders of Kazakhstan and Uzbekistan in Central Asia, was once the fourth largest inland sea in the world. It originally covered 68,000 sq km, but is now half that area, and more than 75 per cent of its water has evaporated.

The sea was once a natural reservoir in a vast desert, and an important fishery. It began drying up in the 1960s, when people diverted the two rivers that flowed into it to use the water for irrigation. The irrigation ditches were poorly constructed and the soil became waterlogged so that the crops of cotton and rice would not grow. Less water flowed into the Aral Sea, and the concentration of salt increased as the water evaporated in the hot sun. This destroyed the fishing industry. Now, there are fishing villages 80 km from the water where fishing boats have been left high and dry.

A fishing boat marooned by the shrinking of the Aral Sea on the borders of Kazakhstan and Uzbekistan in Central Asia.

DRIEST PLACE

The world's driest place is the Atacama Desert in Chile. Rainfall here is barely measurable, averaging less than 0.1 mm a year. Some places in the Atacama have had no rain for more than 400 years.

Sandstorms and dust storms

Sandstorms and dust storms happen during periods of drought. In desert areas high winds lift sand particles into the air and blow a sandstorm across the landscape. This usually happens during the day, when the ground has become hot, and the storms die out at night as the Earth cools down again. The force of the wind-blown sand can etch the glass of windows and sandpaper the paint from vehicles. Over a long period of time sandstorms erode rocks into unusual shapes. The sand particles usually rise no more than 3m above the ground, although occasionally they reach 15m. Millions of tonnes of sand can be shifted in just a few hours and sand from the Sahara has even been blown to the United Kingdom and parts of South America.

A sandstorm in China. Over-intensive farming and climate change have caused deserts to spread in Asia and Africa, affecting millions of the world's poorest people.

Dust storms happen where farmland has been left bare or has dried out during a drought. Rising winds lift the loose, dusty soil and carry it for hundreds of kilometres. A dust storm can be up to 640 km wide, and lift the dust to 4,300m. It can shift millions of tonnes of dust in hours.

Both sandstorms and dust storms look like a coloured wall kilometres high approaching. During a dust storm you cannot see more than 400m ahead. The air is so thick with dust that no living thing can breathe. It blocks roads and railways, enters locked buildings, closed cupboards, food and machines and may hang in the air for days. It filters the Sun's rays, creating beautiful sunsets.

Wildfires, some caused by lightning and some started deliberately by people, are common during drought. This wildfire is destroying eucalyptus woodland in Australia.

Wildfires

Plants become very dry during a drought and wildfires often occur. Hot, dry winds fan the flames. Some wildfires are begun by lightning, but most are caused by people, usually by accident, but occasionally deliberately. Most fires started by lightning are eventually put out by rain. They may die out when they reach water or an area where there is little material to burn. If a wildfire is not controlled, it can rage across the countryside, causing widespread damage and loss of life. Fires also pollute the air with their smoke. In 1997 and 1998, Indonesia and Malaysia suffered their worst drought in 50 years. People used fires to clear areas of forest, but the monsoon rains did not come to put them out. The fires burned out of control for months, covering the area with smoke.

Useful fires

Although fires can damage property and crops, they can also be useful. Fires burn dried plants and dead wood and clear gaps in forests, where new tree seedlings can grow. After a fire in the dry African savanna grasslands, green shoots appear, providing food for grazing animals. Some plants, such as eucalyptus trees and banksia shrubs in Australia, rely on fire to release the seeds from their pods.

Eucalyptus trees sprout new growth three months after a wildfire in Australia.

The American Dust Bowl

Dry, dusty soil unprotected by plants easily blows away. The finest particles blow away first, leaving behind the less fertile larger particles. One of the most famous examples of this occurred in the Great Plains in the United States. During the 1860s, several rainy years transformed this area, which had previously been very dry. The few farmers who had settled there enjoyed good harvests until 1887, when drought struck again.

During the early twentieth century, the rains brought good harvests again. In the 1920s people who had little knowledge of how to farm fragile soils settled on large areas of the natural prairie grassland there. Millions of hectares of grassland in Colorado, New Mexico, Texas and Oklahoma were ploughed and planted with cereal crops. The shallow roots of these plants could not bind the soil, whereas the interlocking roots of the natural grasses formed a mat of roots just below the surface which held the fine soil in place. To increase profits, the farmers grew the same cereal crops year after year, rather than allowing the soil to rest (lie fallow) some years. They also raised cattle which overgrazed the soil. Eventually the overworked soil became dry

PEOPLE AND DESERTS

The United Nations calculates that more than 250 million people suffer from the results of desertification – the spreading of desert conditions – while 1 billion more are at risk.

THE NORTH AMERICAN DUST BOWL

This map shows the huge area of farmland affected by drought during the 1930s in the Great Plains in the United States.

Area affected by dust bowl

Area of greatest soil erosion

400 km

Montana

North Dakota

South Dakota

Wyoming

Nebraska

Iowa

Colorado

Kansas

Missouri

New Mexico

Oklahoma

Arkansas

Texas

A small-scale irrigation project in the Sinai Desert in Egypt. Used carefully, irrigation helps farmers to grow good crops in desert soils.

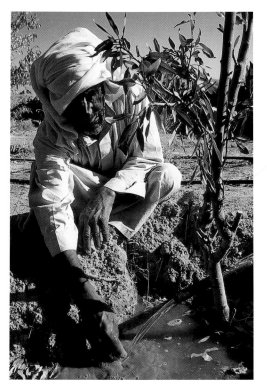

and powdery. In 1932, the Great Plains region suffered a severe drought. Vast areas had low rainfall for almost a decade and for five years there was no rain. Crops failed and fierce storms and hot, dry winds blew away the dry topsoil in swirling clouds.

One gale in 1934 swept across the United States and picked up more than 350,000 tonnes of the dusty soil. Birds suffocated in mid-air and cities such as New York were plunged into darkness when clouds of dust blotted out the Sun. Thousands of farmers were ruined, and more than 350,000 people had to abandon their homes. Thousands more died of starvation, or of lung diseases caused by breathing in the dust-laden air. Relief finally arrived in 1940, when there was heavy rainfall across the region. After similar rainfalls in 1941, the disaster was over, but fewer than half the farmers were left in the region.

Improved farming methods

In 1935 the American government began to improve what had become known as the Dust Bowl. Some land was planted with grasses to bind the soil. Crops were planted in rotation so that they did not damage the soil, and fields were rested every third year. Hedges and windbreaks of trees were planted to lessen the force of the wind. Reservoirs were built to store water. Despite this, every ten years or so, there have been droughts and destructive dust storms when the soils remain vulnerable. In Russia, too, dry areas of the steppes were ploughed and planted with cereal crops after the Second World War, and similar severe dust bowl erosion occurred.

Modern drought precautions

Drought cannot be predicted reliably, but there are precautions that can be taken if the money is available to pay for them. Reservoirs can be built to store water when it does rain, and irrigation channels dug to carry this water to crops. Terraces can be cut into sloping fields, or ridges of stones laid across them, to prevent rainwater running away down slopes.

Drought-resistant trees, such as acacias and eucalyptus trees, can be planted as windbreaks and to stop soil blowing away. Crops grow strongly in the shade of the trees, which eventually provide valuable firewood. Putting animal manure and compost on dry soils helps them to hold water longer. These materials also bind the soil particles together and prevent them from blowing away. Farmers can learn about the dangers of overcropping and overgrazing, and governments can try to prevent people settling in drought-prone areas.

Ice and snow

8

A landscape blanketed by pristine white snow is
a beautiful sight. Plants with a sparkling coat of frost
can look equally attractive. But ice and snow can bring
traffic to a standstill and can be deadly to people.

Blizzards

A combination of heavy snowfall, low temperatures and strong winds
creates a blizzard. A snow storm is called a blizzard if the wind speed
is greater than 56 kph. A blizzard can bring whole cities to a standstill.
As well as disrupting transport, it brings down power lines, leaving
whole communities without electricity. A blizzard which dumped
120 cm of snow on the east coast of the United States in February
2003 left more than 225,000 people without electricity. People with
no other means of heating or cooking, begin to suffer from hypothermia.
Those at greatest risk are babies and old people.

The storm of the century

North America suffered a blizzard which earned the title of the storm
of the century in March 1993. Satellite images showed a huge mass of
cold air moving down from the north polar regions. When it reached the
Gulf of Mexico, it collided violently with warm, moist air in the region.

*New Yorkers struggle
through a snowstorm
on foot.*

The storm that resulted swept across Cuba, bringing torrential rain, hurricane-force winds and mountainous waves. About 1,500 houses were destroyed and 37,000 badly damaged.

The storm then turned north and grew colder. Florida was battered by fierce winds and unusually heavy snowfalls. The blizzard moved up the south-eastern side of the United States, powered by winds of up to 200 kph. Heavy snowfalls collapsed roofs and brought down power lines. In the state of North Carolina, storm surges wrecked beachfront houses and 152 cm of snow fell on the Appalachian Mountains.

In the northern United States and Canada people were better prepared. But 25 cm of snow brought New York City to a standstill and the major airports in the eastern United States were closed. The 1993 blizzard was responsible for 243 deaths and caused $3 billion damage. This would have been much worse had weather forecasters not been able to give early warning of the storm's arrival.

Large parts of the United States were again brought to a standstill by a blizzard in January 1996. The state of Philadelphia was buried under over 76 cm of snow, while New York received at least 51 cm, and 23 people died. A blizzard on New Year's Eve 2000 blanketed New York and New Jersey with 40 cm of snow, bringing widespread disruption.

WET OR DRY SNOW?

As a general rule, 25 cm of snow produces the same amount of water as 2.5 cm of rain. But different types of snow vary. When snow is very dry and powdery at low temperatures, 76 cm is equivalent to 2.5 cm of rain. When snow is soft and wet and falls at a temperature just above freezing point, as little as 10 cm of snow is equivalent to 2.5 cm of rain.

Mediterranean blizzards

From time to time blizzards affect countries bordering the Mediterranean Sea. In February 2004, blizzards cut off 2,700 villages in Turkey. Two ships sank off the Turkish coast near Istanbul with the loss of 20 lives. The neighbouring countries of Bulgaria and Greece were also badly affected, and 50 cm of snow fell on the Greek capital, Athens.

Ice storms

Ice storms are formed when rain that has fallen through warmer air meets a layer of very cold air near the ground. The rain does not have time to change to sleet. Instead, it turns to ice when it touches any solid object.

In January 1998, a severe ice storm lasting five days raged through eastern Canada and the north-eastern United States. More than 220,000 people lost their power supply in the state of Maine alone. The ice destroyed 2,500 pylons and brought down thousands of kilometres of power cables. Falling trees and icy roads made travel impossible. In eastern Canada, the storm brought down 129,000 km of cables along with 1,000 pylons, leaving three million people without power.

Frozen vegetation after an ice storm in Central Oklahoma in the United States.

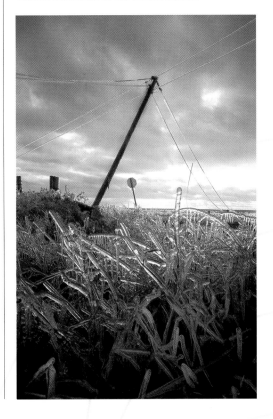

How avalanches are caused

The most dramatic killer in cold climates is the avalanche. A huge mass of snow, usually mixed with ice, soil and rock, rushes down a mountain destroying everything in its path. An avalanche creates a strong wind on either side which can be powerful enough to uproot trees.

Avalanches begin high on mountains above the snow-line, where temperatures are below freezing, so that fresh falls of snow pile up, rather than melting. As more and more snow accumulates, its weight turns the lower layers into ice, which begins to slide down the mountainside. On steep slopes, the ice layer can be eroded by spring rains or a rise in temperature as the winter snows begin to melt. A sudden, heavy fall of snow which does not have time to stick to the rock, ice or snow beneath it can also set off an avalanche.

An avalanche sliding down a mountainside can be extremely powerful and can reach speeds of 320 kph. Avalanches can kill people even inside their homes. This happened to the inhabitants of the village of Ozengeli in Turkey when an avalanche hit in January 1993. Rescuers dug out 21 survivors, but 53 died in the rubble and snow.

During the winter of 1999, the Austrian Alps had mild weather followed by heavy snowfalls and strong winds. A block of snow, probably weighing 170,000 tonnes, broke away from the side of a mountain and crashed on to the village of Galtur below. More than 30 people were killed.

Types of avalanche

There are two main kinds of avalanche. In very cold, dry weather, light powdery snow grains do not stick together. If this type of snow starts to move down the mountain,

A massive powder avalanche crashes down a mountain near the ski resort of Telluride in south-west Colorado.

INSIDE AN AVALANCHE

To study avalanches from the inside, scientists in Montana in the United States have built an underground lookout post on a mountain slope. With the help of explosives, they set off an avalanche. As it rushes down the mountain, the avalanche passes over the lookout, from where the scientists film and study it. One of their findings is that the temperature of the avalanche material increases as it slides down the mountain. The further the avalanche has travelled, the greater the increase. The aim of the research is to learn how to forecast avalanches accurately.

it forms a powder avalanche that swirls along like a huge white cloud. A slab avalanche is more dangerous, and it starts off as a solid chunk of frozen snow about the size of a football pitch and about nine metres deep. This sort of avalanche often forms when sunny days are followed by frosty nights, so that melted snow freezes again.

Limiting the damage

Every year about 100 million tourists and skiers visit the European Alps. Avalanches kill about 150 of them. In the United States avalanches have killed more than 500 people since 1950. As more people enjoy winter sports in the mountains, the need to anticipate avalanches is growing. Trained snow patrols carry out 'snow profiles' to predict avalanches. By looking closely at the snow layers and their temperatures, guides can estimate how stable the packed snow is. When snow and ice are precariously balanced, even a small vibration can trigger an avalanche. A sudden gust of wind, or noises such as a loud shout or thunder can set one off. When an avalanche threatens, explosives or rockets can be used to bring it down. A small, planned avalanche is easier to deal with than a large, unexpected one. At the slightest danger, warnings are broadcast and roads and ski-runs closed.

FRESH SNOW

The risk of an avalanche is greatest when fresh, loose snow falls on to a layer of frozen snow. The slightest disturbance will cause a huge block of newly-fallen snow to slide into the valley below.

This concrete tunnel protects a road from avalanches in Central Switzerland.

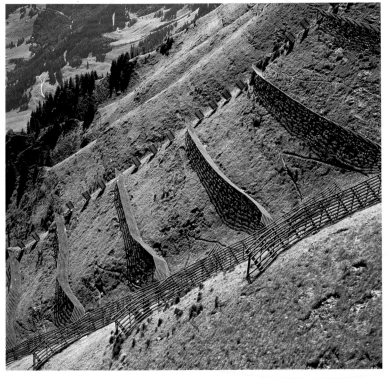

These metal fences are designed to break up any avalanche forming on the slopes of this mountain in Mannlichen, Switzerland.

9

El Niño

Oceans have a major effect on weather and climate, and none more so than the Pacific. Here, a current of warm water in the Pacific Ocean which usually flows east changes direction every two to seven years. This causes extreme climate change in parts of the world.

DROUGHTS

The growth of the world's deserts and the long drought in Africa's Sahel region have been blamed on global warming. Scientists now believe these events were partly due to El Niño.

An El Niño event

In a normal year, trade winds blow from east to west across the equatorial part of the Pacific Ocean and push water warmed by the tropical Sun west. The waters on the western side of the Pacific may be more than 10°C warmer than on the east. Over the warm water, the air pressure is low, and lighter, moist air rises to bring clouds and heavy rain to South-East Asia, New Guinea and northern Australia. On the eastern side, where the seawater is cold, air pressure is high. Few clouds form, so little rain falls on the western coasts of South America.

When an El Niño event occurs, the current reverses and flows further south, causing the cold area in the eastern Pacific and the warm western area to swap. The pressure reverses and the trade winds weaken or reverse direction. The warm water moves east along the Equator towards the South American coast, where it spreads north and south. On the western side of the Pacific, no rain falls, and there is drought. India, the Sahel, southern Africa and Brazil also have drought.

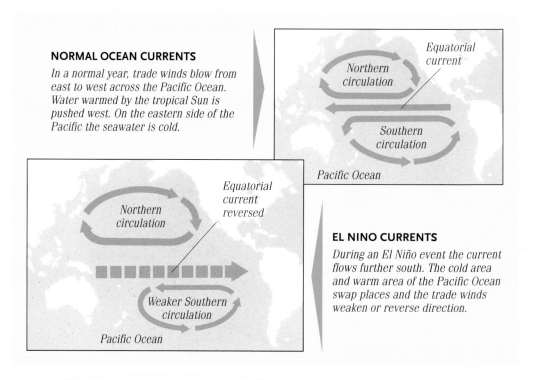

NORMAL OCEAN CURRENTS

In a normal year, trade winds blow from east to west across the Pacific Ocean. Water warmed by the tropical Sun is pushed west. On the eastern side of the Pacific the seawater is cold.

Northern circulation

Equatorial current

Southern circulation

Pacific Ocean

Equatorial current reversed

Northern circulation

Weaker Southern circulation

Pacific Ocean

EL NINO CURRENTS

During an El Niño event the current flows further south. The cold area and warm area of the Pacific Ocean swap places and the trade winds weaken or reverse direction.

Floods and typhoons

El Niño has effects worldwide because changes in ocean temperature bring about changes in the atmosphere. The warm surface water heats the air above, encouraging storms, typhoons and hurricanes. There are droughts in some parts of the world, and increased rain in others, with floods and mudslides in northern Peru, Ecuador and California. At the same time, the northern US has a warmer and drier winter than usual.

El Niño also affects fisheries and wildlife along the coast of South America. Here cold waters rich in nutrients well up from the bottom of the Pacific along the coast. The nutrients provide food for plankton, which in turn feeds fish and other wildlife. In an El Niño year, the warm surface water along the coast of South America prevents the nutrient-rich water rising to the surface. There is less food for the fish, which die or migrate to colder waters in search of food.

La Niña

An El Niño event is often followed by a period of unusual cooling in the tropical eastern side of the Pacific Ocean. This is called La Niña and its effects are the opposite to El Niño, though just as extreme. Extra-strong winds push more warm surface water than usual west towards Indonesia. Around the Americas, cold, deep seawater rises to fill the space. Less evaporation takes place, so rainfall and storms are less frequent in the east but more frequent over the warm waters of the western Pacific.

Corals are especially sensitive to the temperature of seawater. This coral has been bleached (and killed) by the warming of the Indian Ocean around the Maldive Islands.

What's behind El Niño events?

No one really knows what causes El Niño events. Some scientists believe that global warming is the cause, and you can read about this in *Changing Climates*, another book in this series. Other scientists argue that the phenomenon has been around for thousands of years, so could not be caused by recent global warning. There are many conflicting opinions about this: some scientists believe that there is no such thing as La Niña, and that the weather at this time is just normal.

Recent El Niño reverses began in 1984, 1991, 1994, 1997 and 2003. The effects of the changed pattern can last for up to four years. The El Niño event of 1997 was the most extreme of the twentieth century. Indonesia and other parts of South-East Asia suffered the worst drought in 50 years, followed by massive forest fires. Australia also suffered severe drought and bushfires.

A chain of buoys now stetches across nearly one third of the world in the tropical Pacific. They collect information on ocean temperature and winds which is fed into computers to help scientists give early warnings of an El Niño event. Perhaps they may eventually also help to explain this complex and potentially devastating weather pattern.

Glossary

air pressure The force of the air pressing down on the Earth's surface.

anticyclone A large area of high pressure (sometimes called a high) from which all winds blow outwards.

atmosphere The blanket of gases around a planet, held there by the pull of the planet's gravity.

avalanche A rapid movement of snow, sometimes combined with ice and rock material, down a steep slope.

barometer An instrument for measuring air pressure.

blizzard Severe weather conditions which combine heavy snow, strong winds, low temperatures and poor visibility.

climate The average weather in a place over a long period of time.

clouds Masses of water droplets or ice particles floating in the atmosphere. There are ten types, with three basic groups: stratus, cumulus and cirrus.

condensation The process by which a vapour or gas changes into a liquid as it cools.

current A body of air or water moving in a definite direction.

cyclone (see hurricane)

deforestation The permanent removal of forests.

depression An area of low pressure, sometimes called a low, which brings unsettled weather. It may also be called a cyclone.

dew point The temperature at which water vapour in the air condenses.

doldrums A belt of calms or very light winds, but with occasional sudden storms, near the Equator.

drizzle Light rain that is made of drops that are less than 0.5 mm in diameter.

drought A long period of dry weather, with no rainfall.

evaporation The process by which a liquid is changed into a vapour or gas when it is heated.

fog A cloud that has come down to ground level and which has reduced visibility to less than a kilometre.

forecast (weather) A statement of how the weather is likely to change in the future in a particular place.

frost White ice crystals that form on cold surfaces when moisture from the air freezes.

global warming The warming of the Earth's atmosphere due to air pollution.

greenhouse effect The warming of the Earth, caused by certain gases in the atmosphere, called greenhouse gases. These allow the Sun's rays to reach the Earth's surface, but trap heat given off by the ground.

hail Rounded pellets of ice that fall from cumulonimbus clouds.

humidity The amount of water vapour present in the air.

hurricane A violent tropical storm in the Caribbean and North Atlantic with winds blowing at 120 km/h or more around a low pressure centre. It is known as a typhoon in the north-western Pacific and a cyclone in the Indian Ocean and around Australia.

Ice Age One of several periods in the Earth's history when huge glaciers and ice sheets covered large parts of the land surface.

ice storm A storm in which falling rain freezes as soon as it touches any object on the Earth's surface which is below freezing point.

meteorology The study of how the atmosphere creates the weather and climate.

mist A cloud resting on the ground or sea which reduces visibility to between 1 and 2 km.

monsoon A wind which blows from different directions at different times of the year, causing wet and dry seasons, particularly in southern Asia, northern Australia and western Africa.

polar front The boundary (or front) between warm tropical air and cold polar air in the middle latitudes north and south of the Equator. Frontal depressions form and travel along it.

precipitation Any form of water (solid or liquid) that falls from the atmosphere and reaches the ground.

prevailing wind The main direction from which the wind blows in particular places.

rain shadow An area of decreased rainfall on the lee, or sheltered, side of a hill or mountain.

relative humidity The ratio between the actual amount of water vapour in the air and the maximum amount it can hold at a given temperature.

relief rainfall Rainfall resulting from hills and mountains causing clouds to rise and cool.

satellite A moon or spacecraft that moves in an orbit around a planet.

sleet A mixture of snow and rain, or partially melted snow.

snow-line The lowest level on a mountain above which snow never completely disappears.

stratosphere The layer of the atmosphere that lies above the troposphere.

temperature A measure of how hot or cold something is.

tornado An intense, rotating column of air, shaped like a funnel, column or rope, that extends downwards from the base of a cloud to the ground.

trade wind Steady winds in the tropics blowing from the north-east in the northern hemisphere and from the south-east in the southern hemisphere.

tree-line The upper limit of tree growth on a mountain.

troposphere The layer of the atmosphere that lies closest to the Earth. This is where our weather occurs.

typhoon (see hurricane)

vacuum A completely empty space; a space without any air in it.

water cycle The continuous circulation of water from the Earth's surface to the atmosphere, involving evaporation, condensation and precipitation.

waterspout A rotating column of air that extends downward from the base of a cloud to touch a water surface. It is usually less violent than a tornado.

water vapour Water in the form of an invisible gas.

weather What is happening in the atmosphere at any particular time and place in terms of clouds, humidity, sunshine, temperature, visibility, precipitation, air pressure and wind.

wind chill The sensation that the air temperature is lower than it really is because of the cooling effect of the wind on the human body.

Index